PYTHON
FOR BEGINNERS
LEARN IT AS EASY AS PIE

+ CHEAT SHEET

A STEP-BY-STEP GUIDE
TO BUILD 4 SMASHING PROJECTS:

CALCULATOR
DRAWING APP
LOG-IN SYSTEM
NOTES APP

YATIN BAYYA

Python for Beginners: Learn It as Easy as Pie
Copyright © 2020 By Yatin Bayya

ISBN: 978-0-578-77180-9 (Paperback)
ISBN: 978-0-578-79225-5 (Hardcover)
ISBN: 978-0-578-79224-8 (eBook)

First printing edition November 2020

Author's Note

I am a certified Python programmer. Since I was nine years, I have been fascinated with programming. This book will help students, workers, and even entrepreneurs to begin understanding the complexities and opportunities in programming in a step-by-step, easy to follow manner. In a well thought out and meaningful way, I delve into building four functional projects: calculator, drawing app, log-in system, and notes app.

I have found that many people now see the importance of programming and the desire to build projects. Python for Beginners—Learn It as Easy as Pie fills that need; it is a fantastic source that will help guide you in building four projects and broaden your understanding of programming as a skill.

Very likely, you will feel my fascination and creative potential (beyond these four projects) in programming after you finish reading this book.

Thanks to my dad for seeing the potential and his immense support. And thanks to you for picking up this very book. I am looking forward to writing more books and develop more apps.

Table of Contents

Preface

Building a functional, interactive interface from fundamental elements on the blank canvas of a screen is an art. Small, modular parts made from basic building blocks come together to create a structure known as a program.

As of writing this book, I am a 12-year-old middle school student living in the San Francisco Bay Area, who has been exploring and learning various programming languages for the past three years. The atmosphere of tech startups and giants here in the Bay Area had inspired me to start programming with encouragement from my dad.

This world of programming is a vast, endless landscape. Yet it is a beautiful one.

Python is a high-level, object-oriented, general-purpose programming language. Lower-level programming languages are harder to read, while higher-level programming languages are easier. Object-oriented programming languages revolve around classes and objects—a concept that will be covered later. General-purpose programming languages can be used for anything and are not limited to one programming genre. Python is very rich in libraries—external code that a developer like you can use—which means there are almost limitless possibilities for what you can do with it.

This book will take you through the essentials of creating simple projects in a concise approach without any prior programming knowledge.

CHAPTER 1:

Introduction

The digital age is revolutionizing the world in terms of technology and software. Programmers provide the most useful software, enhance the world, and communicate with computers by thinking creatively.

Python is the language of choice for many of these next-generation problem-solvers. It is a powerful language whose explicit syntax allows new programmers to focus on developing software. As of 2020, Python is one of the most popular programming languages and ranks consistently at the top.

This book teaches the essential concepts and syntax of Python 3 and provides guidance for implementation with tutorials on building projects.

Getting Started

Without further ado, here is how to install Python 3 and get started creating applications.

To begin the installation, go to the "Downloads" page on the Python website (https://www.python.org/downloads). Select the latest stable download version (versions 3.x) for your operating system. Open the file after the download completes.

On Windows:

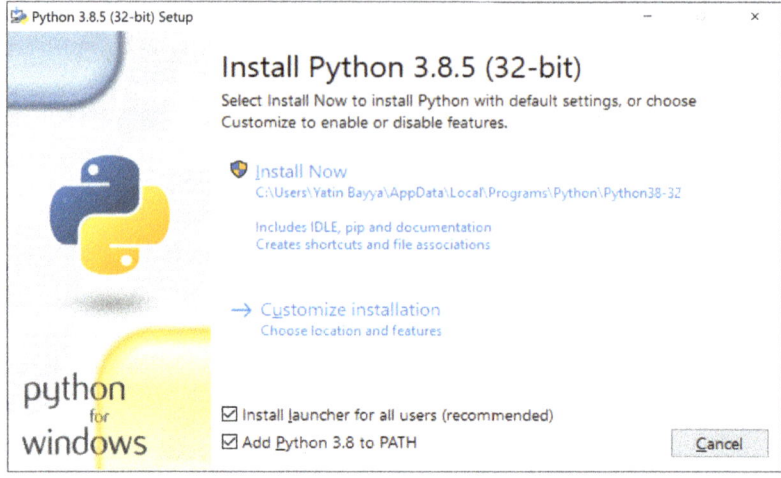

In this window, check "Add Python 3.8 to PATH" and click "Install Now."

On macOS:

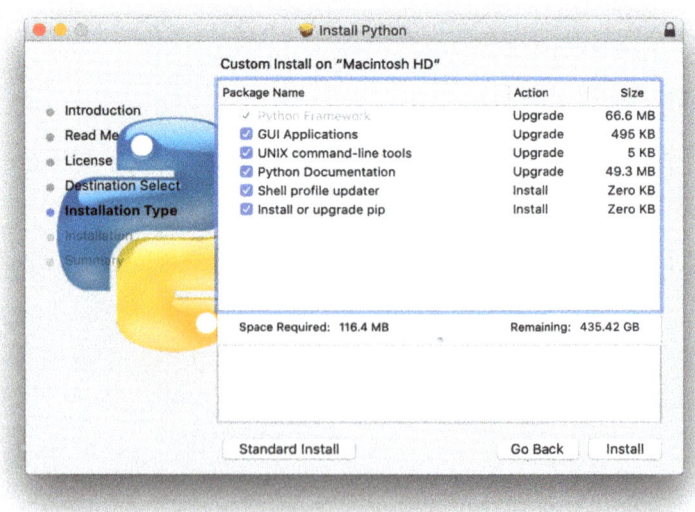

In this window, go through all the steps until "Installation Type" and then click on the button "Customize" and make sure that everything is selected as shown in the preceding window. After you have confirmed, everything is selected, finish the installation.

Once completed, search for the Integrated Development and Learning Environment (IDLE) application which is installed with Python earlier:

This is known as an interpreter, which evaluates and converts the code typed in there on the fly. Python is a high-level programming language that is easier for developers to read. In contrast, the computer understands the low-level machine code that is more difficult to read. The solution for the computer to understand Python is to convert this high-level code into machine code. There are several implementations (ways of converting code) to achieve this:

The first option is to use a compiler that translates the code into machine code and then runs it. The machine code created by the compiler is executable, which can be run on other computers but is not fully cross-platform compatible. The executable cannot run on any operating system unless the source code is shared, and each operating system has its own version.

Another way is to use an interpreter that translates the code on the fly and then runs it, rather than saving a separate file. The downside is that when the application needs to run on someone else's machine, the source code is exposed. Additionally, the client will need an interpreter to run the code. This approach is often slower than compilers because it requires to recompile every single time.

Both options have advantages and disadvantages, but the intermediate approach or bytecode combines their benefits. A virtual machine converts the source code to the lowest level possible while remaining cross-platform compatible. When running it, the compiler translates it into machine code. This code is not executed by the CPU but rather by the Python Virtual Machine (PVM). Python takes this approach, but its process is still, primarily "interpreted," and it also has some compilations under the intermediate approach or bytecode.

In the IDLE menu bar, click on the "File" button and then on the "New File" option:

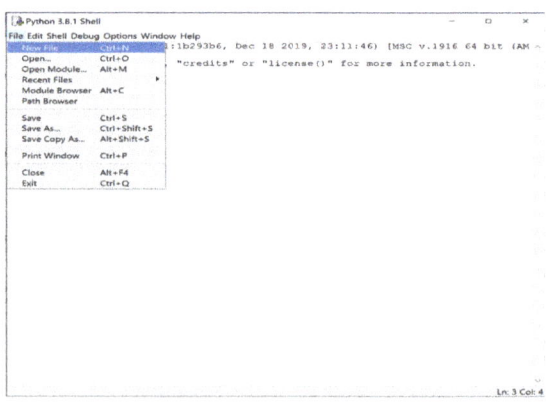

This will open a blank window for Python code. The first program will be a simple program that displays "Hello World" when executed:

```python
print("Hello World")
```

Click on the "Run" option and then "Run Now," and save the file to execute the code. Now it should show the printed result of "Hello World," where commands execute and receive a result. "Print" is a built-in function. A *function* is a block of code that can be executed by using its name. Python's source code defines a function to display a message and calls it to print. Essentially, the "print" function code outputs and displays a *string* (text).

The "print" function's syntax is as follows: *print, parentheses, opening single/double quote, the message, the matching closing quote, closing parentheses*. The message in the function must be enclosed in quotes because that differentiates code from text. Adding comments to code helps developers from a readability perspective, but the interpreter ignores them:

```
print("Hello World") #This prints hello world
```

The *octothorpe* (#) denotes a comment, and all the text on the right-hand side is commented out—or not executed—and acts like plain text, doing nothing.

The code is syntax highlighted. Meaning it color codes keywords and certain distinct parts of the code, in IDLE and other text editors or integrated development environments (IDEs). Although it is possible to type Python code in any program that edits text, text editors and IDEs provide niche features. A *text editor* is simply a program that allows the user to type text with some syntax highlighting ability, while an *IDE* is similar but must also offer feature-rich programming tools for the developer.

Any text editor or IDE can be used for the purposes of this book, but, PyCharm is recommended.

Installing and Using PyCharm

PyCharm is an application that executes Python programs. Download the "Community" version (https://www.jetbrains.com/pycharm/download) and follow through the installation process. Once it is installed, go through these steps:

1. Create a Project.

    a. Give it a name.

    b. Be sure to uncheck the "Create a main.py welcome script."

2. In the project:

    a. Check whether the interpreter is selected there:

        i. On Windows:

        Click "File" on the menu and go to "Settings."

        ii. On macOS:

        Click on "PyCharm" on the menu and go to "Preferences."

        iii. Search for the "Python Interpreter" and open it.

        iv. Select the Python version installed:

    b. Create a new Python file and give it a name.

        i. Open that file.

        ii. In the file, call or use the print function to display "Hello World."

        iii. Right-click and run the application.

        iv. "Hello World" should appear in the bottom window.

It is recommended to create a new Project for every program you write. Each project should have related files that all come together to create a program.

Using the Interpreter

When IDLE is opened without choosing a file, it will open an interpreter, which can also be accessed by typing in "python" to the Terminal (macOS/Linux) or Command Prompt (Windows) application, which should be already on your system.

The Python code, entered in the interpreter, will be *evaluated* or executed on the fly:

Windows Command Prompt:

C:\User\Your Username> python

Output:
Python 3.8.5
Type "help", "copyright", "credits", or "license" for more information.
>>>

macOS/Linux Terminal:

$ Python

Output:
Python 3.8.5
Type "help", "copyright", "credits", or "license" for more information.
>>>

Following the ">>>", is where the code can be typed to execute on the fly:

Windows Command Prompt/macOS or Linux Terminal:

Python 3.8.5
Type "help", "copyright", "credits", or "license" for more information.
>>> print("Hello World")

Hello World

As seen in the last page, the code is executed on the fly and the output is given immediately.

CHAPTER 2:
Variables and Data

A variable is a name with an automatically assigned allocated memory location that refers to a value. In simpler terms, variables are pointers that refer to values. These values fall under a *data type*, or a particular kind of data item, including numeric, textual, Boolean, and "None" types. The proceeding code declares or initializes a variable called "my_variable" and assigns its value to 0:

```
my_variable = 0
```

The left-hand side of the equal sign is the name of the variable. In contrast, the right-hand side is an expression that gets evaluated to a single, independent value. A function called "type" can determine the data type of the value:

```
print(type(my_variable))
```

Output:
<class 'int'>

The above code's output shows that the variable is the type of "class 'int.'" The output means that "my_variable" is an object of the integer class. A *class* is a blueprint that contains the guidelines and properties of an *object*, which is an implementation of a class. In other words, the class provides the rules for what the object is. Every variable in Python is an object, and its data type is its class.

Multiple variables can be sequentially defined in a single line using the following syntax:

> my_variable1, my_variable2, my_variable3 = 1, 2, 3

Multiple variables can also be given the same value in a single line:

> my_variable1 = my_variable2 = my_variable3 = 3

When declaring a variable, the variable is equal not to the expression but rather to the expression evaluated. Therefore, variables are assigned and reassigned independently. See this behavior illustrated below.

```
my_variable1 = 5
print("my_variale1 = "+str(my_variable1))
my_variable2 = my_variable1 + 5
print("my_variable2 = "+str(my_variable2))
my_variable1 = 15
print("[After Change] my_variable1 = "+str(my_variable1))
print("[After Change] my_variable2 = "+str(my_variable2))
```

Output:
```
my_variable1 = 5
my_variable2 = 10
[After Change] my_variable1 = 15
[After Change] my_variable2 = 10
```

As shown in the above output, a variable's value is evaluated and assigned at the time of declaration.

These functions printed concatenated data. *Concatenation* occurs when two or more pieces of data are joined together as one piece of text. When concatenating, the added data must be a string. The "str" constructor—a function that creates an object of the particular data type and the "str"—converts the variables into a string by wrapping them in its parentheses. The strings are then concatenated or combined into one.

10

"None" is a value for variables that do not have a set value at the initialization (when a value is set). Note that the variable will still be an object but one of "NoneType." Below defines a variable with a value of "None":

```
my_none_variable = None
```

Python is a dynamically typed language, meaning variables can change into any data type. In contrast, statically typed programming languages require a declaration of the data type when defining a variable, which can only have values that fall into that data type.

The following table shows the conventions and restrictions for a variable name:

Restrictions	Conventions
Variables must start with an underscore or letter.	Variable names should be in Snake case, where underscores separate different words (e.g., "my_variable" or "snake_case")
The name must only consist of letters, numbers, and underscores.	Variables should be entirely lowercase unless they are constants.
	Variables that should not be touched by anyone else viewing the code should have double underscores on both sides of their names. These are called dunder variables.

Numeric Data: Integers, Floats, and Complex Numbers

Numeric data fall into three types. The two most used types are *integers*, which are whole positive or negative numbers, and *floating points* (*floats*), which are numbers with a decimal point. The last type is *complex numbers*, which are numbers expressed in the form $a + bj$, where a is the real part, b is the imaginary part, and j is the square root of negative one. Examples of the above-mentioned data types are:

```
my_integer = -10
my_float = -10.0
my_complex = 10+5j
```

Numeric values can vary in quantity. An expression could be based on the previous value of the variable or composed of entirely different values. *Arithmetic operators*, or signs that denote functions, can be used to create numeric expressions.

Below is a table of the arithmetic operators, the function each denotes, and what that function does:

Python Arithmetic Operators			
Operator Sign	Operator Name	Denoting Function	Computation
+	Addition	.__add__()	Returns a sum
-	Subtraction	.__sub__()	Returns a difference
/	Division	.__truediv__()	Returns a quotient as a float
//	Floor Division (Int Division)	.__floordiv__()	Returns a quotient floored as an int

Python Arithmetic Operators			
Operator Sign	Operator Name	Denoting Function	Computation
*	Multiplication	.__mul__()	Returns a product
**	Exponentiation	.__pow__()	Returns a power
%	Modulus	.__mod__()	Returns the remainder of a division problem

All these arithmetic operators would return an int unless the expression involved a float, in which case they would also return a float.

The *division operator* always returns a float, but in floor or integer division, it returns an integer. The modulus operator might be the most unfamiliar, but all it does is calculate the remainder of a division. It is primarily used to calculate whether a number is even or odd.

Below is an expression with arithmetic operators.

```
goal = 1000
today = 25
yesterday = 50
progress = today + yesterday
print("Progress Completed: "+str(progress/goal)+"%")
```

Output:
Progress Completed: 0.075%

Behind the scenes, when "today + yesterday" gets evaluated, it calls the function "today.__add__ (yesterday)."

The final "print" statement in the preceding code consists of multiple arithmetic operators. However, it is adding strings, or textual data, rather than integers. In the string constructor, it converts "progress/

goal" into a string. But "progress/goal" calls "progress.__truediv__ (goal)" for calculation. That gives the output of 0.075.

Expressions are often mistaken for assignment:

```
my_number = 10
my_number + 5
print(my_number)
```

Output:
10

The output is 10 because, in the second line, "my_number + 5" was evaluated but not assigned to "my_number."

Assignment of this expression would look like this:

```
my_number = my_number + 5
```

Because "my_number" is already defined and needs to modify itself with an operation, it is allowed to use the other *assignment operators* that shorten this repetitive process, shown in this table:

Assignment Operators	
Operator	**Computation**
+=	Adds the expression to the variable
-=	Subtracts the expression from the variable
/=	Divides the expression by the variable
//=	Floor divides the expression by the variable
*=	Multiplies the expression by the variable
**=	Calculates the power of the variable with the expression
%=	Divides the expression by the variable and sets the variable to the remainder

Assignment operators calculate their respective arithmetic operator with the variable and assign it:

```
incrementor = 0.0
incrementor += 1
print(incrementor)
```

Output:
1.0

Textual Data: Strings

A *string* is a series of characters surrounded by either double or single quotation marks:

```
my_string = "Hello World"

print(my_string)
```

The *plus operator* (+) concatenates or joins strings (and only strings) together:

```
hello = "Hello"
world = "World"
print(hello+" "+world+"!")
```

Output:
Hello world!

Concatenation only works with strings; therefore, the values joining must convert to a string before being used:

```
high_score = 500
print("High Score: " + str(high_score))
```

Output:
High Score: 500

The constructor "str"—a particular function for the string class to create a string object—wraps around "high_score." In other words, "str" converts the given value to a string, if possible.

Note that string concatenation is not the same as addition. For example:

```
one = "1"
print(one+one)
```

Output:
```
11
```

The variable "one" is equal to the string literal "1" versus the numeric literal "1" (a *literal* is an expression with a single value). These two are entirely different because they are different data types with different behaviors. The string literal "1" would be taken in as any other string and would join the two strings together, outputting "11."

Integers can multiply strings by using the *multiplication operator* (*):

```
my_multiplied_string = "Hello!" * 5
print(my_multiplied_string)
```

Output:
```
Hello! Hello! Hello! Hello! Hello!
```

Depending on which character started the string, a single or double quotation mark inside the string will end. A string can contain the inverse quotation mark that started it:

```
quotes_in_quotes = "He said 'hi'"
```

This way works, but the same quotation mark sometimes must be used. To denote that the quotation mark is not the ending the string, escape characters come in useful. Proceeding this is a table of the most used escape characters:

Escape Characters	
Escape Character	**Result**
\"	A double quotation mark
\'	A single quotation mark
\\	A backslash
\n	A new line
\t	A tab

Using an escape character is as simple as inserting it into a string:

```
my_escape_characters = "This is a double quotation mark: \".\
nUsing this escape character: \\\""
print(my_escape_characters)
```

Output:
This is a double quotation mark: ".
Using this escape character: \"

The output it gave contained a double quotation mark and a backslash using escape characters. A single backslash denotes that an escape character is coming and a double backslash is the escape character for a single backslash.

Strings are indexed, meaning each character can be accessed using its index. The index of the first character is 0 (not 1), and from then on, it increments as the characters increment. For example, this is how the string "Hello World" might be indexed:

H	E	L	L	O		W	O	R	L	D
0	1	2	3	4	5	6	7	8	9	10

That is how indexing works, and this is the syntax for it:

```
hello_world = "Hello World"
print(hello_world[1])
```

Output:
e

The variable name and square brackets with the index comprise the syntax. Indexes can also be negative, where the last character's index is −1. Below is another example with the string "Hello World":

H	E	L	L	O		W	O	R	L	D
−11	−10	−9	−8	−7	−6	−5	−4	−3	−2	−1

The implementation is the same for positive indexes. However, *string slicing* is another concept where a range of characters is selected based on their index:

```
print("Select a range of characters in me"[9:15])
```

Output:
range

If the index is too large or the index range does not fit, an "IndexError" will occur. The index must always be within the range of the characters.

The "len" function retrieves the number of characters or the length of the string:

```
my_string_length = "This is how many characters I have"
print(len(my_string_length))
```

Output:
34

The string class has useful *methods* (functions that are part of a class) that perform specific tasks. One such method, "upper," turns the full string uppercase:

```
my_string = "turn me into uppercase"
my_string = my_string.upper()
print(my_string)
```

Output:
TURN ME INTO UPPERCASE

Another one turns it lowercase:

```
my_string = "TURN ME INTO LOWERCASE"
my_string = my_string.lower()
print(my_string)
```

Output:
Turn me into lowercase

This method below returns a new string with the words replaced:

```
my_string = "Replace me"
my_string = my_string.replace("Replace", "This method changed")
print(my_string)
```

Output:
This method changed me

When the "replace" method is called, "my_string" does not change the string but instead returns a new string with that value. To change the string to that value, it must be reassigned to the string that the "replace" method returns. Above, it reassigns the string to the value returned by the method.

An *f-string* or *formatting string* is a way of inserting data into a string:

```
high_score = 1000
my_string = "Your high score is {high_score}".format(high_
score=1000)
print(my_string)
```

Output:
Your high score is 1000

The value given for "{high_score}" replaces it in the string. This method also allows for inserting sequentially:

```
greeting = "{}, {}".format("Hello", "Python")
print(greeting)
```

Output:
Hello, Python

Unlike concatenation, the inserted data type does not matter.

The string does not need to be formatted immediately, so it is possible to insert new data later.

The syntax for this gets repetitive, but there is a shorthand way to achieve the same task:

```
my_int = 5
f_string = f"I inserted this integer: {my_int}"
print(f_string)
```

Output
I inserted this integer: 5

An f-string is recognized when the letter *f*, denoting it, starts a string, as shown above. Additionally, the f-string looks for the braces and inserts the data specified inside them. In this example, "my_int" was the variable name specified in the braces.

True or False Values: Booleans

Booleans have only two values—*true* or *false*:

true = True
false = False

These are the only values a Boolean can evaluate. However, there are many ways to generate an expression for evaluation. One option is to use *comparison operators*:

Comparison Operators	
Operator	Computation
==	Returns whether the two comparisons are equal
!=	Returns whether the two comparisons are not equal
>	Returns whether the first comparison is greater than the next
<	Returns whether the first comparison is less than the next
>=	Returns whether the first comparison is less than or equal to the next
<=	Returns whether the first comparison is greater than or equal to the next

The examples below demonstrate comparison operators in practice:

my_boolean1 = 5 == 5
my_boolean2 = 3 < 2
my_boolean3 = "a" > "z"

"my_boolean1"is true because the expression "5 == 5" evaluates to that true value. Note that double and single equal signs are different. A double equal sign is a comparison operator, while a single equal sign is an assignment operator. Comparison operators evaluate a simple true or false value, and assignment operators set or change the value of a name.

"my_boolean2" asks whether 3< 2 is true; because it is false, "my_boolean2" will also be false.

"my_boolean3" is false because *z* has a higher American Standard Code for Information Interchange (ASCII) value than *a*. This will only compare the first two different characters in each of the strings.

Another way of generating *Boolean conditionals* (*Boolean expressions*) is through identity operators:

Identity Operators	
Operator	**Computation**
Is	Returns whether the object is in the same memory location
Is not	Returns whether the object is not in the same memory location

The *is* and *double equal* (==) operators are different. The former checks whether they both point to the same object or memory location, and the latter checks whether the values are the same:

```
my_string1 = "hello"
my_string2 = "hello"
my_boolean1 = my_string1 == my_string2
my_boolean2 = my_string1 is my_string2
print(f"[Double Equals] {my_boolean1}\n[Is] {my_boolean2}")
```

Output:
[Double Equals] True
[Is] True

Both conditionals returned true because both strings have the same value and the same memory location. Strings are *immutable*, meaning the value cannot be changed, but the reference of the value can. In other words, immutable variables point to a value that cannot change; only the location can change. Every data type included so far is immutable.

Membership operators check whether a given value is in an *iterable* (a value that can be indexed, such as a string), which includes:

Membership Operators	
Operator	**Computation**
In	Returns whether a value is in an object
Not in	Returns whether a value is not in an object

Below demonstrates the membership operations in practice:

```python
my_boolean = "hello" not in "hello world"
print(my_boolean)
```

Output:
False

Logical operators combine two conditionals:

Logical Operators	
Operator	**Computation**
And	Returns true when both operations are true
Or	Returns true when either operation is true

Here are some examples:

```python
my_boolean1 = 6 > 3 and 4 < 1
my_boolean2 = 6 > 3 or 4 < 1
print(my_boolean1)
print(my_boolean2)
```

Output:
False
True

"my_boolean1" is false because both of the conditionals in the expression must be true for it to be true too.

"my_boolean2" is true because it only requires at least one expression to be true.

Boolean expressions are not the only ones to have a truthy or falsy value. *Truthy values* are considered true and *falsy values* are considered false when converted to a Boolean. Empty strings, collections (more about these in the next chapter), numeric values equivalent to zero, false Boolean expressions, and "None" are all falsy values. "False" is a Boolean value, while falsy values have a default value of "false" when converted; truthy values likewise have a default value of "true." The rest of the data types are all truthy. These values can turn into Booleans to show their truthiness or falseness:

```python
is_string_true = bool("Yes")
is_number_true = bool(0)
print(is_string_true)
print(is_number_true)
```

Output:
True
False

Collections

Collections or *data structures* consist of more than one item, any data type, or any *nested data structure/collection* (a collection in a collection). Different situations require different data structures. All changeable collections are *mutable*, meaning the value changes rather than the place to which a name points. Every variable pointing to that value will also change.

Note that there can be any data type in a collection, including another collection of the same or another type.

Lists

Like strings, *lists* are indexed by items rather than characters. An *item* is simply an indexed value separated by commas. Lists are defined using square brackets:

```
my_list = ["Item 0", "Item 1", "Item 2", "Item 3"]
print(my_list)
```

Output:
```
['Item 0', 'Item 1', 'Item 2', 'Item 3']
```

During initialization, the items of a list do not need to be defined, resulting in an empty list with a falsy value:

```
empty_list = []
```

Indexing lists is the same as strings, but each index is an item rather than a character:

```
my_list = ["Item 0", "Item 1", "Item 2", "Item 3"]
print("Index 3: "+my_list[3])
print("Index -2: "+my_list[-2])
print("Indexes 1-3: "+str(my_list[1:3]))
```

Output:
Index 3: Item 3
Index -2: Item 2
Indexes 1-3: ['Item 1', 'Item 2']

As seen above, each indexed item is a string, so it does not need to be converted to print with another string. Nevertheless, when it comes to a range, a list of items in the range of indexes is returned. Indexing is universal for all indexed collections.

There are four ways to append one or more items to a list:

```
my_list = [1,2,3]
my_list.append(4)
my_list += [5,6]
my_list.extend([5,6])
my_list.insert(0,0)
```

The first adds only a single item, the second, and third add multiple items, and the fourth adds a specific index. The information in the parenthesis for the "insert" method are the index and the value, respectively. There are also two ways to delete a list:

```
no_strings_here = [1, 2, "two", "three", 3, 4]
no_strings_here.pop(2)
no_strings_here.remove("three")
print(no_strings_here)
```

Output:
[1, 2, 3, 4]

The "pop" method deletes it by the index or by the last item if the index were not provided. The "remove" method deletes it by the first occurrence of the value rather than the index.

Lists are mutable, so each index's value can change like this, whereas strings are immutable and must bind a new string to change values:

```python
my_list = ["Item 0", "Item 1", "Item 2", "Item 3"]
my_list[0] = "Apples"
my_list[1] += ": Grapes"
print(my_list)
```

Output:
['Apples', 'Item 1: Grapes', 'Item 2', 'Item 3']

Reassigned immutable variables will never affect any other defined variables:

```python
x=5
y=x
x=3
print(y)
```

Output:
5

With mutable variables such as lists, the value changes rather than the point of reference:

```python
my_list1 = [1, 2, 3, 4, 5, 6, 7, 8, 9, 10]
my_list2 = my_list1
my_list1.append("Numbers")
print(my_list2)
```

Output:
[1, 2, 3, 4, 5, 6, 7, 8, 9, 10, 'Numbers']

The following defines "my_list" for the demonstration of the methods and functions in the proceeding table.

my_list = [5, 9, 3, 5, 7, 9, 1, 2]

Below are the *built-in functions* of a list and other collections:

Built-in Functions of Collections		
Function	**Computation**	**Example**
Sum	Returns the sum of all the items in a numeric list	print(sum(my_list)) 41
Min	Returns the smallest numeric value or ASCII code	print(min(my_list)) 1
Max	Returns the greatest numeric or ASCII code	print(max(my_list)) 9
Len	Returns the number of items in a list	print(len(my_list)) 8
Sorted	Returns a new sorted list arranged from least to greatest	print(sorted(my_list)) [1, 2, 3, 5, 5, 7, 9, 9]

The proceeding table contains the methods of a list:

Methods of a List		
Method	**Computation**	**Example**
Count	Returns the number of occurrences of a value	print(my_list.count(9)) 0
Index	Returns the index of the first occurrence of the value	print(my_list.index(5)) 0
Sort	Rearranges the existing list from least to greatest	my_list.sort() print(my_list) [1, 2, 3, 5, 5, 7, 9, 9]

Another method called *clear* removes all the items and is universal across all collections except *tuples* (defined in the next chapter):

```
my_list.clear()
```

This is how to check whether an item exists in a list using Boolean expressions:

```
groceries = ["apple", "banana", "pancakes", "milk"]
my_boolean = "pancakes" in groceries
print(my_boolean)
```

Output:
True

Nested lists, or lists within lists, are defined—as expected—like this:

```
my_list = [[1,2],[2,4]]
```

31

Accessing nested list indexes can be done like this:

```
print(my_list[0][1])
```

Output:
2

Above, the list "my_list" grabs the zeroth index, and in that index is another list. The next index grabs the first index of that nested list. There can theoretically be infinite levels of nested loops.

Strings can be converted to lists using the *split method*, which splits each item based on a character:

```
split_me = "Hello World"
print(split_me.split())
```

Output:
['Hello', 'World']

By default, it will split the string with spaces, but it can include other *separators* or the characters that separate the string:

```
print(split_me.split("l"))
```

Output:
['He', '', 'o Wor', 'd']

The above created a new string item after every "l" in the string.

Tuples

A *tuple* is an immutable collection defined like this:

```
my_tuple = ("Unchangeable item","Unindexed item")
my_tuple = "Unchangeable item","Unindexed item"
```

Styling the tuple with or without parenthesis will create the same object. However, empty tuples need parentheses:

```
empty_tuple = ()
```

A tuple with only one item must have a comma after it:

```
my_tuple = ("One Item",)
```

If there were no comma above, then it would be that single item; in this case, it would have been a string.

Almost all the built-in functions and list methods carry from previous chapters—other than the "sort" method. However, there is still the "sorted" function, which returns a list rather than a tuple.

Unlike lists, tuples are immutable, meaning items cannot be added, removed, or updated with new values. The only way to get around this is to convert a tuple into a list, modify it, turn it back to a tuple, and reassign it to the original variable holding that value:

```
my_tuple = ("Unchangeable",)
my_list = list(my_tuple)
my_list[0] = "Changeable"
my_list.append("It Works")
my_tuple = my_list
print(my_tuple)
```

Output:
['Changeable', 'It Works']

Like the "str" constructor, which is used when other data types combine with strings, the list constructor takes data and constructs or converts it into a list.

Assigning multiple variables to each of the items in a tuple is a common use case employing tuple unpacking and packing. *Packing* a tuple means assigning it a value:

```
person = ("Kris", 16, "Programming")
```

Then that can be *unpacked* into multiple variables:

```
name, age, hobby = person
print(name)
```

Output
Kris

This only works if the number of items is the same as the number of variables. A special syntax takes the remaining values and puts them into a list using an asterisk:

```
name, *remaining = person
print(remaining)
```

Output:
[16, 'Programming']

Sets

Sets are mutable and unordered collections. The code beneath defines a set:

```
my_set = {1,2,3}
```

Sets have no duplicate items, which means only one will be stored:

```
my_set = {1,2,3,3}
print(my_set)
```

Output:
```
{1, 2, 3}
```

Although a set is mutable, the items of the set can only be of immutable types; otherwise, a "TypeError: unhashable type" error occurs because mutable types are *unhashable*. Variables are only hashable when the hash value never changes, which is only true for immutable types. If a variable has a "__hash__" method, then it is hashable:

```
immutable = 1
print(immutable.__hash__())
```

Output:
```
1
```

```
mutable = []
print(mutable.__hash__())
```

Output:
```
Traceback (most recent call last):
  File "<stdin>", line 1, in <module>
TypeError: 'NoneType' object is not callable
```

The variable "immutable" has a hash method that returns the value of 1. But when the "mutable" variable's "__hash__" method is called, it returns an error saying that a "NoneType" is uncallable, which essentially means the method doesn't exist.

There are two methods for adding items to a set:

  my_set.add(4)
  my_set.update([5,6])

The "add" method adds one, and the "update" method adds everything in the iterable provided. For now, think of an *iterable* as collections and strings—data with more than one member, whether different data items or characters. When a string is updated, it adds every unique character of the string.

There are also two methods for removing: "remove" and "discard." The former outputs an error if not present, and the latter does not:

  my_set.discard(10)
  my_set.remove(1)

Frozensets are immutable sets that carry all the same methods other than "add" and "remove" because they are immutable:

  my_frozen_set = frozenset([1,2,3])

Dictionaries

Dictionaries are mutable, unordered, but indexed collections, but regular indexes have no meaning because they are unordered. Therefore, dictionaries use keys to retrieve a value instead:

```
landmarks = {"San Francisco": "The Golden Gate Bridge", "New York": "Statue of Liberty", "Los Angeles": "Hollywood"}
```

Dictionaries consist of key-value pairs separated by commas. A key-value pair consists of the key first, followed by a semicolon and ending with a value. Values are accessed using keys:

```
print(landmarks["San Francisco"])
```

Output:
The Golden Gate Bridge

There is also another way to write the syntax of a dictionary by using its constructor:

```
user = dict(name="Ram", id=1)
```

If the key did not exist, it would output an error. A way around that is to use the "get" method, which will return "None" if not found:

```
print(landmarks.get("San Francisco"))
```

Creating or reassigning values uses this syntax:

```
landmarks ["New York"] = "Manhattan"
landmarks ["Arizona"] = "Grand Canyon"
```

Another way of doing this is to use the "update" method and pass in a dictionary or list of tuples where each tuple contains a key and a value. That list or dictionary will then be combined with the updating "landmarks" list:

```
landmarks.update({"San Francisco": "Painted Ladies"})
```

The dictionary in the "update" method can include either values that already exist or entirely new ones.

The "pop" method removes an item by the key name:

```
landmarks.pop("Los Angeles")
```

The "pop item" method will remove the last inserted item, though:

```
landmarks.popitem()
```

Since dictionaries are mutable, copies of it can preserve previous versions of it:

```
previous_version_of_landmarks = landmarks.copy()
```

The keys of and values can be received like this, respectively:

```
print(landmarks.keys())
print(landmarks.values())
```

Output:
```
dict_keys(['San Francisco', 'New York', 'Arizona'])
dict_values(['Painted Ladies', 'Manhattan', 'Grand Canyon'])
```

A dictionary key is not limited to strings; it can be any immutable value, and the values can be any data type.

User Input

All the data until now was *hard-coded* in, which means it will execute and give the same output every time. *User input* varies and adds more functionality on top of that:

```
user_input = input("Enter something :")
print(user_input)
```

The terminal would display "Enter Something" and would give an option to type. The "user_input" variable stores what the user has typed and the program will then print it into the console. The value from the "input" function can be used like any other string.

Casting

Casting is the conversion of one data type to the other. There are two types of conversion: *implicit* and *explicit*.

One example of implicit-type conversion occurs during the calculation of operations between numeric types. Python will automatically convert the result and the *operands*, or numeric values in a mathematical expression, accordingly.

Explicit type conversion uses constructors. A *constructor* is a special method of a class that constructs or creates an object. These are the constructors:

Constructors	
Data Type	**Constructor**
Integer	int()
Float	float()
Complex	complex()
String	str()
Boolean	bool()
List	list()
Tuple	tuple()
Set	set()
Dictionary	dict()

The last four collections' constructor accepts any iterable (defined later), collection, and string. When strings are passed in, they will turn them into lists by character.

```python
print(list("list"))
```

Output:
['l', 'i', 's', 't']

This concept is the same for all collection constructors.

Printing text with other data types commonly uses the "str" constructor:

```python
print("Integer: " + str(1))
```

Another use case of a constructor is when user input arrives and needs to be another data type:

```python
my_input = int(input("Enter an integer :"))
```

CHAPTER 3:
Control Flow

The control-*flow* statements determine the execution of the program. Each control-flow statement has its own purpose and use case.

Indentations

Indentations indicate the scope (the rules for where data is accessed and/or created) of a program. Indented statements that follow a colon are part of that control-flow statement and execute accordingly. The indented lines of code are collectively called a *code block*, which is ended when the indentations stop. In other programming languages, code blocks are denoted within braces, but they are denoted with indentations in Python. Here is an example:

```
if True:
    pass
```

A code block must have at least one statement in it. "Pass" is a placeholder statement for code blocks because they must have at least one line of code. All the statements that are indented are part of the "if" control flow statement. After the indentation ends, the code block will end.

The "if" may seem unfamiliar, but it will be covered in the next chapter.

If Statements

An "if" statement decides whether to execute its body based on the conditional's truthiness:

```python
if 5==5:
    print("5 equals 5")
```

Output:
5 equals 5

The syntax for the if statement, as shown above, is *if "conditional":*, and an indented body with one or more lines of code. The first thing it does is check whether the conditional is true. If it were, then it would execute the indented lines of code until the indentation stopped. If it were false, then the "if" statement would skip all the indented lines and continue after them.

If the first "if" statement is not true, the program will go to the next immediate "elif" statement, if any:

```python
if "":
    print("Empty strings are truthy")
elif 3 >2:
    print("Three is greater than two")
```

Output:
Three is greater than two

It is the same drill for the "elif" statement; it will execute the indented code if its conditional is true. Nevertheless, if all "if" and "elif" statements fail, there is an "else" statement that executes its code block if none of the above statements are true:

```
if False:
    print("False is True")
else:
    print("None of the above conditionals are true")
```

Output:
None of the above conditionals are true

The conditional in the "if" or "elif" statements accept plain Boolean values, Boolean expressions/conditionals, variables, and other data types. By default, the expression checks the truthiness of the value.

There can also be *nested "if" statements*, which are "if" statements within "if" statements:

```
if True:
    if 5-4 == 1:
        print("5-4 is 1")
    else:
        print("5-4 is not 1")
```

The same concept where the indented lines are part of the body of the enclosing "if" statement still applies.

Loops

Loops repeat blocks of code until the condition is proven false. There are two types of loops: "for" and "while." Each time the code repeats, it is called an *iteration*.

While Loops

A "while" loop keeps repeating its body as long as the conditional is true. The syntax for it is *while conditional*:

```
while True:
    print("This is an infinite loop")
```

Because the above "while" loop's conditional is always true, it will be an infinite loop. Here is an example of a user-controlled "while" loop:

```
keep_repeating = True
while keep_repeating:
    keep_repeating_input = input("Do you want to keep repeating this? [y/n]")
    if keep_repeating_input.lower() == "y":
        keep_repeating = True
    else:
        keep_repeating = False
```

This code will keep asking the user whether they want to repeat the loop. If the lowercase version of what they enter is something other than "y," it will break the loop (get out of the loop) because the conditional will be proven false. There is another way to break out of a loop using the "break" keyword:

```
while True:
    print("The loop is going to break now")
    break
```

Output:
The loop is going to break now

This code only repeated once because, after the one "print" statement, the "break" keyword caused it to exit the loop.

A loop can also have a "counter," which counts the iterations and stops at a certain point:

```
counter = 1while counter < 5:
    print(counter)
    counter += 1
```

Output:
1
2
3
4
5

The code above repeated five times and printed the "counter" for each iteration. The "counter" will often start at zero and work its way to the desired iterations.

Iterables can be iterated over in a loop. They have more than one item, such as strings with characters and collections with indexed members. Each item can be iterated over like this:

```
hello = "Hello"
counter = 0
while counter < len(hello):
    print(hello [counter])
    counter += 1
```

Output:
```
H
e
l
l
o
```

The same concept applies to a list:

```
my_list = ["banana", "grapes", "apples", "cherries"]
counter = 0
while counter <len(my_list):
    print(my_list[counter])
    counter += 1
```

Output:
```
banana
grapes
apples
cherries
```

"While" loops can also have "else" statements that execute once the condition is proven false:

```
i = 0
while i == 1:
    pass
else:
    print("Executes after the condition is proved False")
```

Output:
Executes after the condition is proved False

For Loops

"For" loops are generally used to loop through an iterable (something to be iterated over). There are two ways to do this. The code below demonstrates the first way:

```python
produce = ["apples", "bananas", "grapes"]
for fruit in produce:
    print(fruit)
```

Output:
apples
bananas
grapes

This code will create a new variable called "fruit" with the same value for each item in the list as the "for loop" iterates for each item.

The second way of looping through a data structure is to use a data type called "range":

```python
for i in range(0, len(produce), 1):
    print(produce[i])
```

Output:
apples
bananas
grapes

The "range" constructor creates a range for the counter variable "i" (for "index," commonly used to name a counter variable). The "range" constructor requires the starting point, the stopping point, and the skip count. The *starting point* by default is zero, and the default for the skip count is one. The *skip count* is how much it skips by; in this case, it is "1," and for each iteration, "i" is one more than itself. Because these two are the defaults, all that is needed is the *stopping point* or the time it hits the length of the list:

```
for i in range(len(produce)):
    print(produce[i])
```

Exception Handling

Exceptions are errors. By default, the interpreter will handle an exception by raising it. For example, if a variable name is not defined but is trying to be accessed, it will output a "NameError":

```
print(non_existant)
```

Output:
```
Traceback (most recent call last):
  File "location", line 1, in <module>
    print(non_existant)
NameError: name 'non_existant' is not defined
```

The exception provides this information, respectively: the *location*, *file location*, *line number*, *code*, and *error*. The error message consists of the error name—in this case, "NameError"—and the rest of the exception. Any of these errors can be raised like this:

```
raise TypeError
```

Output:
```
Traceback (most recent call last):
  File "location", line 1, in <module>
    raise TypeError
TypeError
```

Exceptions raised can also have messages:

```
raise TypeError("Message Goes Here")
```

Output:
```
Traceback (most recent call last):
  File "location", line 1, in <module>
    raise TypeError("Message Goes Here")
TypeError: Message Goes Here
```

Exceptions are not user-friendly, so "try-except" blocks are used to prevent these things from showing up. They will try to execute the code, but if they fail, they execute the code in the "except" block rather than raise an exception:

```
try:

    print(5/0)
except Exception:
    print("Dividing by zero is not possible")
```

Output:
Dividing by zero is not possible

This code will work, but it is catching any exception, which is too broad. It is a best practice to catch a specific error instead, such as the one outputted here:

```
Traceback (most recent call last):

  File "location", line 1, in <module>
    print(5/0)
ZeroDivisionError: division by zero
```

The "ZeroDivisionError" is that specific error; ergo, the code must catch it:

```
try:
    print(5/0)
except ZeroDivisionError:
    print("Dividing by zero is not possible")
```

Output:
Dividing by zero is not possible

The output is still the same, but the code gets cleaner. Clean code is essentially code that is easy to understand, read, and change. Don't repeat yourself (DRY) code is one way of cleaning up the code.

There is also the "finally" block that executes after all the "try-except" code, whether there was an error or not:

```
try:
    my_list = []
    print(my_list[1])
except IndexError:
    print("Index out of range")
finally:
    print("I am done")
```

Output:
Index out of range
I am done

When handling exceptions, this block will not usually be based on intentional or accidental mistakes but rather on user input or varying information not controlled by (or unknown to) the developer.

CHAPTER 4:

Building a Project: Calculator

With the basics of Python, the control flow, and the data types, it is possible to create a functional calculator. The first steps are to define the first variables and—optionally—welcome the user:

```
print("Welcome to the calculator")
numbers = []
keep_asking = True
```

The list will store all the numbers that allow the user to input an unlimited amount of numbers. Then there is another variable called "keep_asking" that will be conditional of the "while" loop that asks the user to input more numbers.

Then there needs to be a "while" loop with the conditional or Boolean expression of "keep_asking." This loop will keep looping until the value is false. These tasks below demonstrate what will happen for each iteration:

1. Create a variable called "new_number" which is the number the user entered.

2. Try to append the float version of "new_number" to the list, "numbers."

   a. If the program is unable to convert it into a float, then print that it is unable to do so.

3. If there are more than two numbers in the "numbers" list, then ask the user whether they want to add more numbers.

a. To avoid being casesensitive, the lowercase version of what the user entered is checked to see whether it is equal to "n." If it is, then the"keepasking" variable is set to "False."

This code will do the preceding operations:

```python
while keep_asking:
    new_number = input("Enter a number: ")
    try:
        numbers.append(float(new_number))
    except:
        print("Sorry, this is not a number. Try again.")
    if len(numbers) >= 2:
        keep_asking_input = input("Do You Want to Enter More Numbers? [y/n] ")
        if keep_asking_input.lower() == "n":
            keep_asking = False
```

After the "while" loop execution, the user needs to provide the arithmetic "operation":

```python
else:
    operation = input("Enter an Operation [+/-/*//]: ")
```

Now the program has enough input provided to do the calculations. The "answer" variable will store, well, the answer for each calculation. The first item in the list, "numbers," will initialize the variable "answer."

```python
answer = numbers [0]
```

The "answer" variable is the starting point equal to the first item in the "numbers" list. Then a "for" loop runs through the first index (second item) to the length of the list. The "for" loop next performs the calculations on the "answer" variable:

```
for i in range(1, len(numbers)):
    if operation == "+":
        answer += numbers[i]
    elif operation == "-":
        answer -= numbers[i]
    elif operation == "*":
        answer *= numbers[i]
    elif operation == "/":
        answer /= numbers[i]
```

For each iteration, it will check the "operation" and update the "answer" variable with that number. After these iterations, it will fully calculate the "answer" and displayed to the user:

```
print("The answer is "+str(answer))
```

The project is now complete, and this is the full source code:

```
print("Welcome to the calculator")
numbers = []
keep_asking = True
while keep_asking:
    new_number = input("Enter a number: ")
    try:
        numbers.append(float(new_number))
    except:
        print("Sorry, this is not a number. Try again.")
    if len(numbers) >= 2:
        keep_asking_input = input("Do You Want to Enter More Numbers? [y/n] ")
        if keep_asking_input.lower() == "n":
            keep_asking = False
else:
    operation = input("Enter an Operation [+/-/*//]: ")
answer = numbers [0]
```

```python
for i in range(1, len(numbers)):
    if operation == "+":
        answer += numbers[i]
    elif operation == "-":
        answer -= numbers[i]
    elif operation == "*":
        answer *= numbers[i]
    elif operation == "/":
        answer /= numbers[i]
print("The answer is "+str(answer))
```

CHAPTER 5:

Functions

Functions are blocks of code that can be executed anywhere in the code. One example is the "print" function, which comes defined with Python and is called like this:

```
print("Hello World")
```

Calling a function means executing the code block of a function and passing the information if needed. The function will either return a value or execute something. The information passed in the "print" statement is "Hello World." It takes that value, stores it in a variable, and uses that variable to display it to the terminal window.

Creating Functions

Like variables, functions have names given by the developer. Variables have names that can be accessed and manipulated, and functions have names that can be called and used anywhere in the code. This is how a function is defined:

```
def my_function():
    print("From My Function")
```

The function's name is "my_function," and it's indented contents print "From My Function":

```
my_function()
```

Output:
From My Function

The parentheses after the name are needed; otherwise, they refer to the object of the class function. However, the function will execute its code block with the parentheses.

The "print" function allows the developer to give it a value that will be printed. Each value given when calling a function is an *argument*. The variables created in the function for that argument are called *parameters*. Parameters are defined and used like this:

```python
def my_print_fn(words):
    print(words)
my_print_fn("Hello World")
```

Output:
Hello World

The parameter— "words"—is given to the "my_print_fn," and it prints that parameter. Each parameter is assigned sequentially, butit can alternatively be explicitly defined:

```python
my_print_fn(words="Hello World")
```

Commas separate multiple parameters or arguments:

```python
def add(x, y):
    print(x+y)
add(1, 1)
add(x=1, y=1)
```

Output:
2
2

A parameter can be made optional by providing it with a default value that will be taken unless the arguments override it:

```
def greet(name="User"):
    print("Hello, " + name)
greet()
greet(name="Parin")
```

Output:
Hello, User
Hello, Parin

The "*args" keyword allows the function to have a varying or infinite number of parameters. All the arguments will be members of a list using "*args":

```
def add_all(*args):
    sum = 0
    for number in args:
        sum += number
    print(sum)
add_all(5, 10, 5)
```

Output:
20

The parameter, "*args", can be named anything but must start with an asterisk (*).

This parameter constructs the arguments into a list, and "**kwargs," or keyword arguments, constructs the arguments to a dictionary. The keys will be the names of each argument, and their values will be defined:

```
def person(**kwargs):
    print("First Name: " + kwargs["first_name"])
    print("Last Name: " + str(kwargs["last_name"]))
    print("Age: " + str(kwargs["age"]))
person(first_name="Marut", last_name="King", age=57)
```

Output:
First Name: Marut
Last Name: King
Age: 57

Functions can return values. For example:

```python
def add(x, y):
    return x+y
sum = add(5,5)
print(sum)
```

Output:
10

The variable, "sum" is the value that the "add" function returns.

Recursions, or functions inside functions (nested functions), break down operations:

```python
def get_factorial(x):
    if x == 1:
        return x
    else:
        return x * get_factorial(x - 1)
factorial = get_factorial(5)
print(factorial)
```

Output:
120

The "get_factorial" functions get a *factorial*, the product of the number and its preceding numbers (*e.g.*, factorial 5 is "5*4*3*2*1"), of the parameter "x." The function first checks whether "x" is 1 and then returns the final product if it is, but if it is not, then it returns "x" times the output of "get_factorial" with the same number minus 1.

Say the number given was "3." The function would return "3" multiplied by the output of "get_factorial," with the argument of "x– 1," which is the next number for the factorial. That function would again return itself, but this time with "2" multiplied by "get_factorial" with the argument of "1." It would then return "1" because that would be the last number by which it would need to multiply. When "1" were returned, it would return the result needed for the calculation of "2*1." After that was calculated, it would calculate the previous result, "2," with the original argument of "3," resulting in the value "6," which is the product of "3*2*1." This is essentially what is happening:

1. x=3

2. Returns 3*"get_factorial(3-1)"

    a. "get_factorial(3-1)" returns 2*"get_factorial(2-1)"

        i. Returns 1 since "x" is 1

There is a limit on how deep it can go, which can be received by creating an infinite (in theory) loop:

```
def infinite():
    infinite()
infinite()
```

Output: Traceback (most recent call last):
  File "location", line 3, in <module>
    infinite()
  File "location", line 2, in infinite
    infinite()
  [Previous line repeated 996 more times]
RecursionError: maximum recursion depth exceeded

The exception given was a "RecursionError" because it went 996 layers of functions in the return statement. In simple terms, *recursion* is nothing but repeated computation until the final result is given that would return that result for the previous repeated computation.

The *scope* is the rule for where a variable is defined and assessed, which depends on its location. If it is in the function, it can only be accessed in the function, which means it is a *local* variable; otherwise, it is *global*, or accessible anywhere in the program. Variables defined outside a function can be accessed anywhere, but variables defined in a function only exist within it:

```python
global_variable = "Accessible Anywhere"
def my_scope():
    function_variable = "Accessible Only in Function"
    print(global_variable)
    print(function_variable)
my_scope()
print(function_variable)
```

Output:
```
Traceback (most recent call last):
  File "location", line 6, in <module>
    print(function_variable)
NameError: name 'function_variable' is not defined
Accessible Anywhere
Accessible Only in Function
```

The "NameError" was caused by the sixth line, which was a function that tried to access a nonexistent variable that was unknown outside the scope of the function. Meanwhile, the other messages displayed came from the function, which accessed its inner variable, "function_variable," and the global variable called "global_variable." But this doesn't mean variables initialized in a function must be within the scope if it is possible to make them global:

```
def define_variable_x():
    global x
    x = 1
define_variable_x()
print(x)
```

Output:
1

Variables defined in parameters are also only accessible in the function. Moreover, if that name is the same as a global one, it will pick up the local one. The local and the global name are not the same references nor have the same memory location.

Lambda

"Lambda" functions are single-line functions that return at least one value:

```
my_lambda_function = lambda: 5+5
print(my_lambda_function())
```

Output:
10

"Lambda" functions can also have parameters:

```
my_lambda_function = lambda x, y: x+y
print(my_lambda_function(5,10))
```

Output:
15

These "lambda" functions can optionally have names, but they are called *anonymous functions* if they do not.

The "lambda" function is helpful when using built-in functions such as the following map function, where a new function is unnecessary:

```
my_list = [1,2,3]
my_list_doubled = list(map(lambda item:item*5, my_list))
print(my_list_doubled)
```

Output:
[5, 10, 15]

The "my_list_doubled" variable is equal to a map function with a "lambda" converted into a list. The map function takes a "lambda" expression that considers the parameter of the current list item and returns it multiplied by 5. The "lambda" expression determines each item's value, which is the item multiplied by 5 here. The second parameter of the map function is the list that is going to be edited, which explains the output of "[5, 10, 15]." In most use cases, a default return type is a map object that is not going to be used, with the list being used instead.

The "filter" function returns a modified list too. Instead of editing each item, it will filter the list via a conditional and return a filter object. Only if that conditional is true will it be returned to the list:

```
cities = ["Chicago", "New York", "San Francisco", "Los Angeles",
"Seattle"]
cities = list(filter(lambda city: city [0] == "S", cities))
print(cities)
```

Output:
['San Francisco,' 'Seattle']

CHAPTER 6:

Modules and Packages

A *package* or *library* is a collection of modules that usually has a purpose of providing reusable functionality. Packages are not only reusable in the project but anywhere on the machine. External libraries are built by other developers or institutions to provide a solution. The standard way to install these libraries is through the package manager, pip. Each of them has a specific command to be entered. Python Package Index (PyPi) (https://pypi.org) has most of the pips.

Packages can be installed and uninstalled like this, respectively, in the terminal:

```
pip install package_name
pip uninstall package_name
```

This command will show all the packages installed:

```
pip list
```

A Python file can be called a *module* and imported. Importing packages allows the program to use functions and variables from one or more files in a package.

Say there is a file that needs a file called *b* with the following contents:

File B:

```
def b_file_fn():
    print("Function called from file b")
```

Then there is file *A.py*, in that there are several options to call this method. One way is to import a function from that file:

File A:
```
from b import b_file_fn
b_file_fn()
```

Output:
Function called from file b

This code gets that function from file *B.py*. A star denotes everything so it can import everything from a particular file:

File B:
```
from b import *
b_file_fn()
```

Output:
Function called from file b

Importing functions or variables with another a name is the second way that avoids naming conflicts:

File A:
```
from b import b_file_fn as b_func
b_func()
```

Output:
Function called from file b

A third way is to import the file and refer to it:

File A:
```
import b
b.b_file_fn()
```
Output:
Function called from file b

Importing external libraries and packages is done the same way; the only difference is that the location will be with the other libraries or packages.

CHAPTER 7:
Turtle

Turtle is a library included with Python that provides a blank graphical user interface (GUI) that can be drawn on:

```
import turtle
turtle.mainloop()
```

Output:

This screenshot is the default window of Turtle with no customization. This is displaying because of the method called "mainloop." This method will keep rendering the window until it is closed; otherwise, it would close immediately, but all the customization of the window must be done before the "mainloop" function because everything after it only executes once the window is closed. The "mainloop" function should be called at the last line. Once the window is closed, the turtle window cannot be accessed.

The name and background color of this window can also be changed with the code, respectively:

```
turtle.title("My Window")
turtle.bgcolor("light blue")
```

The "bgcolor" method also accepts a hex color code (a six-digit code composed of numbers and letters for all the colors), a series of letters, and digits that get a specific color.

The pen is the tool that draws on the screen, and it can be customized and controlled using its methods. The below code shows the pen:

turtle.pendown()

This method results in a black arrow in the center of the screen. The method "pendown" is not required to show or use the pen when it is being used. The shape and color of this pen can be customized too:

```
turtle.shape("turtle")
turtle.fillcolor("blue")
turtle.pencolor("white")
```

The shapes that the parameter of a turtle includes are arrow, circle, triangle, and the turtle animal. The fill color is the color of the turtle shape, where the pen color is the outline color and the color that it uses to draw. The turtle pen is at coordinates (0, 0) if not customized, and it can move around the *quadrants* or the areas of the display. This table is how the quadrants look like in a turtle window:

- x coordinate, + y coordinate	+ x coordinate, + y coordinate
- x coordinate, - y coordinate	+ x coordinate, - y coordinate

The above shows whether the *x* or *y* coordinate is positive or negative for each corner relative to the center of the screen. The pen can go to a precise coordinate on the screen like this:

turtle.goto(100, 100)

Output (Including the Previous Code Snippets):

The pen can also be controlled in simple directions such as forward, backward, right, and left. The forward method takes the distance to travel and goes forward in the direction it is facing:

turtle.forward(100)

The following methods turn the Turtle pen toward a direction by degrees:

turtle.backward(90)
turtle.right(90)
turtle.left(90)

Another way to set the Turtle pen is by degrees, where the top of the screen facing is always 90 degrees:

```
turtle.setheading(90)
```

This method sets the direction the Turtle pen faces rather than turning it toward a direction.

The pen can create circles and dots. The former only needs a radius, while the latter needs both radius and color, respectively shown as:

```
turtle.circle(50)
turtle.dot(50, "black")
```

The Turtle draws outlines, but it is also possible to make it fill what it draws like this:

```
turtle.begin_fill()
turtle.circle(50)
turtle.end_fill()
```

Output:

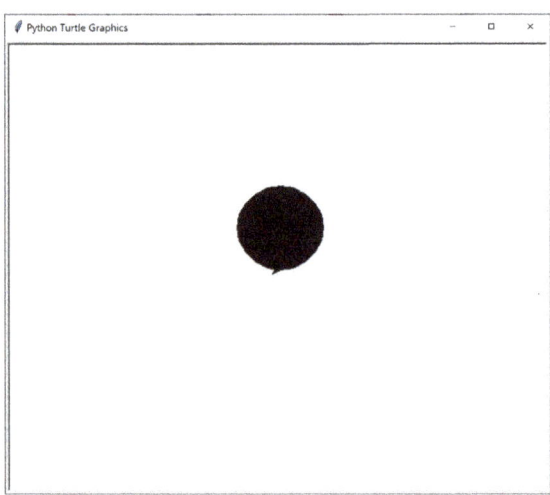

The color of the filling is the *fill color*, or the color used to color the shape of the pen.

The pen can also stop or start drawing like this, respectively:

```
turtle.penup()
turtle.pendown()
```

The speed of the Turtle can go faster:

```
turtle.speed(10)
```

The animation can completely be gone, making the result almost instant:

```
turtle.tracer(False)
```

The Turtle module can create some beautiful designs and patterns with the power of "for" loops:

```
import turtle
turtle.title("My Window")
turtle.speed(500)
colors = ["red", "orange", "yellow", "green", "blue", "purple"]
for i in range(60):
    turtle.pensize(5)
    turtle.pencolor(colors[i%6])
    turtle.circle(10*i)
    turtle.setheading(-i*10)
    turtle.left(i)
turtle.mainloop()
```

Output:

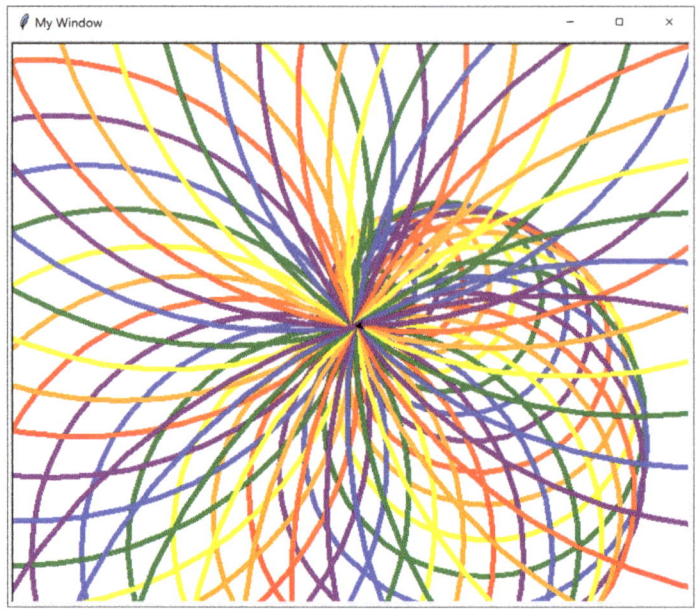

CHAPTER 8:

Building a Project: Drawing App

This chapter will focus on creating a drawing app using the Turtle module. The first steps are importing and creating the Turtle window:

```
import turtle
turtle = turtle.Turtle()
```

For each of the arrow keys, the Turtle must turn and move forward in that direction. The below code is how it will look for the "up" function:

```
def up():
    turtle.setheading(90)
    turtle.forward(10)
```

This function changes the Turtle's direction to 90 degrees, which faces toward the top of the window. Then it will move forward by 10 pixels in that direction. Similarly, these are the remaining directions:

```
def left():
    turtle.setheading(180)
    turtle.forward(10)
def down():
    turtle.setheading(270)
    turtle.forward(10)
def right():
    turtle.setheading(0)
    turtle.forward(10)
```

The screen of the Turtle needs to listen to these events, which are triggered when the user presses a key. To achieve this, create a variable called "screen" before the Turtle is defined, which will avoid the naming confusion:

```
window = turtle.Screen()
```

Instead of rendering the Turtle, the window must:

```
window.mainloop()
```

The window must listen to the key events, and the respective functions should run on the keypress:

```
window.listen()
window.onkey(up, "Up")
window.onkey(down, "Down")
window.onkey(left, "Left")
window.onkey(right, "Right")
```

The user should now be able to draw with the arrow keys on the screen.

This source code is the complete version of the drawing app.

```
import turtle
window = turtle.Screen()
turtle = turtle.Turtle()
def up():
    turtle.setheading(90)
    turtle.forward(10)
def left():
    turtle.setheading(180)
    turtle.forward(10)
def down():
    turtle.setheading(270)
    turtle.forward(10)
def right():
    turtle.setheading(0)
    turtle.forward(50)
window.listen()
window.onkey(up, "Up")
window.onkey(down, "Down")
window.onkey(left, "Left")
window.onkey(right, "Right")
window.mainloop()
```

CHAPTER 9:

Working with Text Files

All user input and data created will only be stored temporarily during *runtime* (during the execution of the code). Writing and saving information on files makes the data permanent. When opening a file, there are several options of mode, but these are commonly used:

Modes	
Name	**Purpose**
R	Reading (default mode)
W	Writing (creates a new file if not already created)
A	Appending (creates a new file if not already created)
r+	Reading and writing

This code shows how to open a file in reading and writing mode after the file is created in the same level directory (the same folder/directory as the Python file):

```
file_data = open("my_file.txt", "r+")
print(file_data.read())
file_data.close()
```

The variable "file_data" opens a file in the reading and writing mode. A file is known as a *resource* and should always be closed after use. If it is not closed, the file takes up memory and might not update with new changes, and other programs cannot access it. Python only sometimes closes files automatically, so it is a best practice to close them.

The proper way to deal with resources is to create a "try-finally" statement. The former block will do the operations with the file, and the latter will close it:

```python
file_data = open("my_file.txt", "r+")
try:
    print(file_data.read())
finally:
    file_data.close()
```

Because this way of dealing with files is common, there is a shorthand technique using *context managers* that automatically closes a file:

```python
with open("my_file.txt", "r+") as file_data:
    print(file_data.read())
```

As seen above, the context manager's syntax is: *with open ("filename", "mode") as name*. The name given to the data refers to the text in the file.

Reading

The "read" method reads the file with one optional parameter of how many characters it should return, but it will be the whole file by default:

```python
with open("my_file.txt", "r+") as file_data:
    print(file_data.read())
```

Another method called "readlines" returns a list of all the lines in a file:

```python
print(file_data.readlines())
```

Each line in a file can also be looped through:

```python
with open("my_file.txt", "r+") as file_data:
    counter = 0
    for line in file_data:
        counter+=1
    print("There are " + str(counter) + " lines")
```

Writing and Appending

In "write" mode, it will create a new file if it does not exist. The "write" method will replace the full file with the new content:

```python
with open("my_file.txt", "w") as file_data:
    file_data.write("Hello World")
```

However, writing to a file in "append" mode will add to the file rather than replace everything:

```python
with open("my_file.txt", "a") as file_data:
    file_data.write("New Content \n")
```

CHAPTER 10

Building a Project: Log-in System

This chapter will teach how to build a log-in system that will give the functionality of logging in and signing up. When signing up, it will hash but can only practically be done one way—the data—and saved in a text file. The first step is to import all the modules needed, which is just a hashing library here:

```python
import hashlib
```

Then the user must be able to sign up:

```python
def signup(username, password ):
    with open("user_details.txt", "a") as user_details:
        user_details.write(username + "," +
hashlib.sha256(password.encode("utf-8")).hexdigest() + "\n")
    print("Account created")
```

This signup function takes two parameters: the username and the password. It opens a resource file, and it will append to the file "user_details.txt." The username is inserted in plain text, followed by a comma and the yet-to-be hashed password. In simple terms, what is happening here is that one of the "hashlib" class methods, "sha256," (a one-way encryption method) takes a byte string (an encoded string or a string converted to another form). Since the password variable is not a byte string, it is encoded, and that method of a string encodes by default to utf-8. Finally, the "hexdigest" method returns the string of the hash. The files append all this and a new line for the next items.

This is the password-protected area for when the user has logged in:

```
def account(username):
    if account_login[username]:
        print("You've Logged in")

    else:
        print("Login Failed")
        login()
```

This function will take a username and check whether the dictionary "account_login" with the key of whatever entered username variable has a truthy value. If it is, then it will prompt a message that the user has logged in; otherwise, it will tell the user the login failed and call the log-in function. For this function to work, there needs to be a global dictionary called "account_login" at the top of the document:

```
account_login = {}
```

Then there needs to be a log-in function:

```
def login(username, password):
    with open("user_details.txt") as user_details:
        for user_detail in user_details:
            if user_detail.split(",")[0] == username and
user_detail.split(",")[1] ==
hashlib.sha256(password.encode("utf-8")).hexdigest():
                account_login[username] = True
                account(username)
    username = input("Username: ")
    password= print("Password: ")
    login(username, password)
```

This function first opens the resource, "user_details.txt," and loops through each line. Then it checks whether the zeroth index of the line split by a comma would be the username and whether the second index would be the hashed version of the password entered. If it would, the function sets the dictionary's key of the username to "true" and calls the function "account" with the username passed in. If none were true, it prompts the user to enter the details again.

All the modular parts—the functions—are completed. Now the program needs to present the options and call that function, accordingly:

```python
def options():
    option = input("Do you have an account? [y/n]")
    username = input("Username: ")
    password = input("Password: ")
    if option == "n":
        signup(username, password)
    else:
        login(username, password)
```

This code creates a function called "options" that asks whether the user has an account and runs the functions accordingly.

The final task is to call the "options" function at the end of the signup and program. The below source code is the complete code after these tasks:

```python
import hashlib
account_login = {}
def signup(username, password):
    with open("user_details.txt", "a") as user_details:
        user_details.write(username + "," +
hashlib.sha256(password.encode("utf-8")).hexdigest() + "\n")
        print("Account created")
        options()
def account(username):
    if account_login[username]:
        print("You've Logged in")
```

```
        else:
            print("Login Failed")
            login()
def login(username, password):
    with open("user_details.txt") as user_details:
        for user_detail in user_details:
            if user_detail.split(",")[0] == username and
user_detail.split(",")[1] ==
ashlib.sha256(password.encode("utf-8")).hexdigest() + "\n":
                login[username] = True
                account(username)
    username = input("Username: ")
    password = input("Password: ")
    login(username, password)
def options():
    option = input("Do you have an account? [y/n]")
    username = input("Username: ")
    password = input("Password: ")
    if option == "n":
        signup(username, password)
    else:
        login(username, password)
options()
```

CHAPTER 11:

Object Oriented Programming

Object-oriented programming consists of four concepts using classes and objects. This approach helps reduce redundancy, cleans up code, and makes it more readable.

Classes and Objects

Classes are like blueprints, and objects are an implementation of them. These blueprints will have certain properties; for example, a car class would have the properties of color, speed, acceleration, and others. It would also have some functionality using functions, which might include driving, braking, and airbags. These properties and functionality will all be part of a class. An object will be one implementation of that class with custom properties. This is how a class is defined:

```python
class Car:
    def __init__(self, speed, fuel):
        self.speed = speed
        self.fuel = fuel
    def drive(self):
        self.speed += 20
        self.fuel -= 5
        print("Driving at " + str(self.speed) + "MPH with " +
str(self.fuel) + " gallons remaining")
    def stop(self):
        self.speed = 0
        print("The car has stopped")
```

The car class ("class Car") consists of two properties ("speed, fuel") and two methods ("drive, stop"). A method is a function in a class. When an object is created, the "__init__" runs.

This code creates a Car object using its constructor, which is in the "__init__" method:

```
my_car = Car(speed=0, fuel=50)
```

All variables in Python are objects of their respective classes; they, too, have constructors that take values to construct an object. This is what the "__init__" method does, and the properties it asks to create an object come in the form of an argument that can be made optional, like how it can be made optional in functions.

The keyword "self" refers to the object or instance of the class; in this case, it refers to "my_car." This keyword avoids confusion between the parameter names and the object names in the methods. The "self" keyword, a period, and then a name define a property of the object created. Every method in a class uses the "self" keyword, which will automatically be provided when called when an object or method is called. In other words, the "self" keyword is the object.

The constructor does not necessarily have to define all the properties of a class. They can also be changed directly like this:

```
my_car.speed = 80
```

The name of the property— "speed" in this example— isn't required to be defined before its assignment; it can be something entirely different. Similarly, methods are called and can be defined outside the class like this, respectively:

```
my_car.drive()
my_car.drive = lambda: "Driving Fast"
```

By convention, all class names must be upper camel case (*e.g.*, "My-Class"). *Camel case* is when the first letter of each new word (not including the first) is capitalized, and *upper camel case* is when the first letter is also capitalized.

YATIN BAYYA

Abstraction

Abstraction refers to hiding certain details and showing only the essential information to the user. For example, radio has an interface with buttons to adjust the volume and channel and to power it. When the user presses the button, it plays the channel. The same can be said of a program. The functionality of single or related classes, objects, and functions can be hidden away in a separate file. The main file can import all of them to use the tools it provides.

In practice, this is how it would be implemented. In a separate file called "dog," create the "Dog" class ("class Dog"), as shown below:

```
class Dog:
    def __init__(self, breed, size, age):
        self.breed = breed
        self.size = size
        self.age = age
    def bark(self):
        print("Bark! Bark!")
    def nametag(self):
        print("I am a" + str(self.age) + " year old " + self.size + " "
+ self.bread +)
```

Then in the main file, "animals," import the other file:

```
from new import Dog
my_dog = Dog(breed="Chihuahua", size="Small", age=2)
my_dog.bark()
```

The code behind the "Dog" class is hidden or abstracted but still usable via an object.

Encapsulation

Encapsulation increases security and simplicity by restricting access to certain methods and properties of a class. Implementing this is as simple as adding a double underscore in front of a method or property:

```python
class SecureUser:
    def __init__(self, username, password):
        self.username = username
        self.__password = password
    def __login(self):
        print("You've logged in")
me = SecureUser(username="Kris", password="123")
print(me.__password)
me.__login()
```

Output:
```
Traceback (most recent call last):
  File "location", line 8, in <module>
    print(me.__password)
AttributeError: 'SecureUser' object has no attribute '__password'
```

As seen above, it will act as if the attribute or property of it didn't exist; even when the eighth line is commented out, it will *throw*(give) the same error:

Output:
```
Traceback (most recent call last):
  File "location", line 8, in <module>
    me.__login()
AttributeError: 'SecureUser' object has no attribute '__login'
```

Implementing encapsulation is easy. Hiding the variables is just a matter of adding a double underscore in front of the name. The class is the only way to refer to a private variable or function using that name.

Inheritance

Inheritance refers to a child class borrowing methods and properties from its parent. Inheritance is used when there are variations of a class that still share many of the same properties. Here is an example:

```python
class Car:
    def __init__(self, speed, fuel):
        self.speed = speed
        self.fuel = fuel
    def drive(self):
        self.speed += 20
        self.fuel -= 5
        print("Driving at " + str(self.speed) + "MPH with " + str(self.fuel) + " gallons remaining")
    def stop(self):
        self.speed = 0
        print("The car has stopped")
class ElectricCar(Car):
    def __init__(self, speed, battery):
        super().__init__(speed=speed, fuel=None)
        del self.fuel
        self.battery = battery
    def drive(self):
        self.speed += 10
        self.battery -= 5
        print("Driving at " + str(self.speed) + "MPH with " + str(self.battery) + "% remaining")
```

The "Car" class ("class Car") is a parent class and can have different variations of itself. The "ElectricCar" class ("class ElectricCar") is a child of the "Car" class, meaning that all the properties and methods get carried over if not overridden. In the "ElectricCar" constructor, the "super" keyword refers to the parent constructor. The code "super.__init__ ()"

calls the "_init_" method of the parent class with the required parameters. Then the "fuel" property is deleted because that property does not work with the "ElectricCar" class. Finally, the "battery" property is created from the parameter in the constructor. Methods can also be overridden, like how the "drive" method does something different depending on the object (*i.e.*, child or parent).

The keyword "super" refers to the parent class and is useful when calling methods from it. As a result, it inherits everything, and the constructor and all the methods copy over to the child class. A parent class can have many children.

Overriding is the concept where a child replaces a method of its parent.

Polymorphism

Polymorphism refers to a method that can take multiple forms. A concept called *duck typing* is one way to achieve this. Duck typing derives from the adage, "If it talks like a duck and walks like a duck, it is a duck," which is also known as the *duck test*. The below code shows polymorphism in action:

```python
class Bird:
    def quack(self):
        print("I am a bird quacking")
class Duck(Bird):
    def quack(self):
        print("I am a duck quacking")
def quack_fn(quacking_animal):
    quacking_animal.quack()
quack_fn(Bird())
quack_fn(Duck())
```

Output:I am a bird quacking
I am a duck quacking

There is only one "quack_fn" function, but it does something different depending on the object passed in the parameter. The only requirement for the object passed in is that it must have a "quack" method; otherwise, it will run into an error. The "Bird" and "Duck" objects are entirely different. However, Python is dynamically typed; it does not require a variable to be locked to a specific data type. If it were, then the parameter's data type would need to be specified, and only one class of objects could be passed in.

Another way of performing polymorphism is to use repeated conditional statements:

```python
def add(a=None, b=None):
    if a == None and b == None:
        return 0
    elif a == None:
        return b
    elif b == None:
        return a
    else:
        return a+b
```

Depending on the conditionals checking the parameter, the above code does something different.

All operators have their functions, and each function does something different depending on the class. For example, the int class ("class int") overrides the method "__add__"—a method that executes whenever two objects are added. That overridden method will add the numbers. Overriding the built-in functions that execute on an operator is also possible:

```python
class TestScore:
    def __init__(self, score):
        self.score = score
    def __add__(self, other):
        print("Sum", end=": ")
        return self.score + other.score
test1 = TestScore(90)
test2 = TestScore(85)
print(test1+test2)
```

Output:
Sum: 175

The preceding code created two objects of class "TestScore." When they were added, it ran the "__add__"method (see *Numeric Data:*

Integers, Floats, and Complex Numbers for more), it printed the sum and ended the print statement with a colon instead of a new line. Finally, it returned the sum, 175, or the "TestScore" properties added. Before overriding this method, this error would occur if the method were not overridden:

```
Traceback (most recent call last):
 File "location", line 9, in <module>
  print(test1+test2)
TypeError: unsupported operand type(s) for +: 'TestScore' and
'TestScore'.
```

CHAPTER 12:

More Python

Iterator and Generator Expressions

Iterators are functions that take an iterable or a class that has "__
iter__"and"__next__" methods and iterate over it:

```
nums = [1, 2, 3]
my_iterator = iter(nums)
print(my_iterator.__next__())
print(my_iterator.__next__())
print(my_iterator.__next__())
```

Output:
1
2
3

The iterator, "my_iterator," is an "iter" object and takes the parameter of an iterable, "nums." It goes to the next item every time the "__next__"method is called, but it will give an error if the amount of iterations is higher than the number of items in a list. Another way of iterating is by using the "next" function:

```
print(next(my_iterator))
```

Iterators can also take in classes if they can iterate and get a value:

```
class Incrementor():
    def __init__(self, number):
        self.number = number
```

```
    def __iter__(self):
        return self
    def __next__(self):
        previous_number = self.number
        self.number += 1
        return previous_number
my_incrementer = Incrementor(1)
iterable = iter(my_incrementor)
print(iterable.__next__())
print(iterable.__next__())
print(iterable.__next__())
```

The class created is "Incrementor," which is initiated with a number and has two methods, "__iter__" and "__next__." The "__iter__" method returns itself to initiate the iterator. Any form of the "__next__" method on the iterable will call the "__next__" of the object. This method will also add the numbers to the "Incrementor" object.

The functions "any" and "all" use generator expressions to check whether a conditional is true for just one item or all the items, respectively and each returns a Boolean. The below code will check whether all the list items are even:

```
numbers = [10, 6, 2]
all_numbers_even = any([number % 2 == 0 for number in numbers])
print(all_numbers_even)
```

Output:
True

The "any" function's parameter is a *generator expression* or *list comprehension*, which saves more memory. However, in simple terms, it needs a conditional followed by a "for" loop statement with no body or semicolon. The conditional is checked against every number and returns true if one of them passes, as it did here. The same can be said for "all," but it requires everything to be true instead of only one item for it to return true.

Closures and Nested Functions

Nested functions are functions that are enclosed by another function, such as "inner" in this example:

```
def outer():
    def inner():
        pass
```

Closures consist of outer and nested functions with a return statement, with the former returning the nested function:

```
def make_add_function(a):
    def add(b):
        return a + b
    return add
my_add_fn = make_add_function(5)
print(my_add_fn(3))
```

Output:
8

The variable "my_add_fn" is equal to the "make_add_function" given the parameter of "5." The variable "my_add_fn" is a function that returns the "make_add_function."Therefore, "my_add_fn" has a value of the "add"function returned from the "make_add_function." This means "my_add_fn" is just another name for what "add" does, but it adds the parameter *a* that was given to the "add" function.

Decorators

Decorators add more computation and finally return the function's value or execute it. Here, the decorator returns the "inner_function," which checks whether the denominator is 0. If it is, it will print "infinity"; otherwise, it will return the function that was passed in—the divide function. That inner function prints "infinity" if the parameter *b* is 0. If it is not, it will return the result of the function that was passed in with those parameters—the "divide" function. When the user tests this with the numbers 1 and 0, it will print "infinity."

```python
def divide(a, b):
    return a / b
def check_denominator(function):
    def inner_function(a, b):
        if b == 0:
            print("Infinity")
        else:
            return function(a, b)
    return inner_function
divide = check_denominator(divide)
divide(1, 0)
```

Because this is a common use case, there is a simpler syntax to create this decorator: the "at" sign followed by the name of the function that should precede it:

```python
@check_denominator
def divide(a, b):
    return a/b
```

CHAPTER 13

GUI: Tkinter

T*kinter* is a GUI library that comes with Python if checked during installation. A GUI is a window that has buttons, labels, text, and more. In contrast, the previous projects and chapters had a command-line interface in the terminal. Tkinter creates a screen that can be filled with *widgets* (elements of a user interface), which are either packed in or laid out in a grid format of rows and columns. This code creates and renders a new window:

```
from tkinter import *
root = Tk()
root.mainloop()
```

Output:

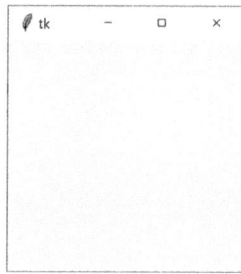

This imports everything from Tkinter. Then it creates a variable called "root," which is an object of "Tk" (the *window object)*. Finally, the "mainloop" method of "root" is called, which keeps looping to render the window (*i.e.*, it keeps the window open).

Tkinter can be imported another way too:

```
import tkinter
root = tkinter.Tk()
```

The disadvantage of this option is that Tkinter must refer to every function, class, and variable.

Here is another way it can be imported:

```
import tkinter as tk
root = tk.Tk()
```

This option changes the name of "tkinter" into "tk." The name "tk" can be used to call its methods and variables like an object. For the rest of this chapter, it will be imported as to how it was in the first code.

With this empty canvas, there can be extra widgets such as the *label widget*—a widget that displays text to the screen:

```
from tkinter import *
root = Tk()
my_text = Label(root, text="Hello World")
my_text.pack()
root.mainloop()
```

Output:

This code creates a label widget called "my_text," which is part of the screen, or "root," and has the text of "Hello World." This widget is then packed into that window "root." When the window is rendered, it will show all the widgets packed.

The title of the window is "Tk," which is visible when expanded, but that is changeable by calling the function:

```
root.title("My Window")
```

Another property of "root" that is changeable is "geometry" (height xwidth):

```
root.geometry("600x300")
```

The window is "resizable," and this function can change that:

```
root.resizable(height=False, width=False)
```

All code after the "mainloop" will only execute after the window is destroyed (closed). Before that, configuring widgets is possible:

```
my_text = Label(root, text="Hello World")
my_text.pack()
my_text.config(text="Text Changed")
root.mainloop()
```

Output:

Any of the properties are configurable as long as the configuration occurs before the window is destroyed.

The label widget has many more properties than the window and the text; here are additional parameters that also apply to other widgets:

Widget Properties	
Parameter	**Parameter Value**
Text	String
Foreground/fg (text color)	String(color)
Background/bg	String(color)
Width	Integer
Height	Integer

This code shows all the above properties in action:

```
my_text = Label(root, text="Hello World", background="black",
foreground="white", width=50, height=10)
my_text.pack()
```

Output:

Another property is the "font," which takes the font's family, size, and style:

```
Label(root, text="Hello World", font=("Arial", 50, "bold"))
```

There are also many other kinds of widgets, such as the entry and button widgets. The "Entry" widget is a field that allows the user to enter text in:

```
username = Entry(root)
username.pack()
```

At any point, the program can see the text in the "Entry" widget:

```
username.get()
```

A button press can indicate when the user has finished inputting the details in those "Entry" widgets,as shown below:

```
submit = Button(root, text ="Login", command=print("logged in"), bg="black", fg="white")
submit.pack()
```

The "command" parameter requires a function, which will run when the user presses the button.

There is also another widget called "Combobox" that is, essentially, a drop-down list:

```
from tkinter import *
from tkinter import ttk
root = Tk()
dropdown = ttk.Combobox(root)
dropdown ["values"] = ["1","2","3"]
dropdown.pack()
root.mainloop()
```

Output:

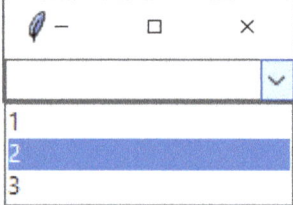

The "ttk" module is separately contains more widgets with extra con-figurability, and "Combobox" is one of them. The drop-down values are given in the form of a list of strings. To set the default value of a drop-down list, use the "current" method, which takes the parameter of the index number in the values:

dropdown.current(0)

The value of the drop-down list can be received like this:

print(dropdown.get())

Instead of items packed in the preceding window, the window can con-tain items laid out in a grid format:

item.grid(row=1, column=1)

Items can also be placed at an exact coordinate with the "place" meth-od, which takes x and y coordinates, where the top left corner is (0,0):

item.place(x=50, y=50)

Previously, the first parameter was the master "root." However, within the Tkinter window, there can be multiple frames carrying multiple items:

```
frame = Frame(root)
frame_txt = Label(frame, text="Frame 1")
frame_txt.pack()
frame_btn = Button(frame, text="Click Me",
command=print("From the Frame"))
frame_btn.pack()
frame.pack()
```

The Tkinter documentation (https://docs.python.org/3/library/tk.html) has plenty more Tkinter widgets.

The "TopLevel" widget creates a child window that closes once the other window does:

```
child_root = Toplevel()
```

For the most part, this "TopLevel" widget will act as a regular Tkinter window. A program can also have multiple regular Tkinter windows by simply defining another one:

```
root2 = Tk()
```

Every widget has to be laid out in a grid or packed in, but it cannot be both. With the grid, this is how to create a basic log-in form:

```
from tkinter import *
root = Tk()
root.title("Login")
username = Entry(root)
username_label = Label(text="Username: ")

password = Entry(root, show="*")
password_label = Label(text="Password: ")
```

```
submit = Button(root, text="Submit")
forgot = Button(root, text="Forgot Password")
username_label.grid(row=1, column=1)
username.grid(row=1, column=2)
password_label.grid(row=2, column=1)
password.grid(row=2, column=2)
submit.grid(row=3, column=1)
forgot.grid(row=3, column=2)
root.mainloop()
```

Output:

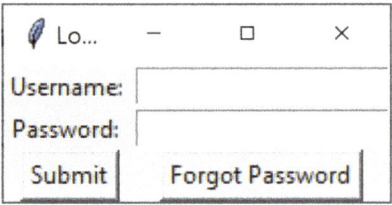

CHAPTER 14:

Building a Project Notes App

The core functionality of the notes app, covered in this chapter, is an option to open, edit, and save a file with the help of these modules:

```python
from tkinter import *
from tkinter import filedialog
from tkinter import scrolledtext
```

This window will be the starting screen of the app:

This screen is composed of one frame—an object of a custom-made class, "StartingScreen":

```python
class StartingScreen(Frame):
    def __init__(self, master, *args, **kwargs):
        super(StartingScreen, self).__init__(*args, **kwargs)
        self.master = master
        self.title = Label(self, text="Notes", font=("Arial", 20),
justify='center').pack()
        self.open_btn = Button(self, text="Open a File", width=20,
command=self.open_file, justify='center').pack()
        self.pack()
    def open_file(self):
```

```
file = open(filedialog.askopenfilename())
editor = Editor(self.master, file.read()).pack()
self.destroy()
```

The "StartingScreen" is a child class of its parent "Frame." Therefore, it inherits all the methods and variables. In the "StartingScreen" constructor, it calls its parent constructor and passes in the "*args" and "**kwargs" parameters. These parameters allow unlimited arguments and named arguments, which are then passed into its parent constructor or the "Frame" widget.

This widget will take care of all the other customization or extra parameters. It then sets properties for the object, such as "master," "title," and "open_btn." The "master" property is the parent of a widget, or where the widget is added. "Master" is usually the first parameter, "root," or the name of a frame. The "title" widget is a label widget that says "Notes," and the "open_btn" widget is a button that opens a file using the "open_file" method.

The "filedialog" imported earlier comes into play in the "open_file" method. This module has a method called "askopenfilename," which returns a file of what the user had picked when prompted. With this data, it creates an object called "Editor" with the parent's details and the file's content and packs it in. After this, it destroys itself (essentially deleting itself). Before the "StartingScreen" class is defined, create the editor class with the following code:

```
class Editor(Frame):
    def __init__(self, master, content, *args, **kwargs):
        super(Editor, self).__init__(master, *args, **kwargs)
        self.menu = Menu(self.master)
        self.file_menu = Menu(self.menu)
        self.file_menu.add_command(label="New",
```

```
        command=self.back_to_start)
            self.file_menu.add_command(label="Save",
        command=self.save)
            self.file_menu.add_command(label="Exit",
        command=root.quit)
            self.menu.add_cascade(label="File", menu=self.file_menu)
            self.master.config(menu=self.menu)
            self.text = scrolledtext.ScrolledText(self)
            self.text.insert(1.0, content)
            self.text.pack()
            self.pack()
        def back_to_start(self):
            root.config(menu=Menu(root))
            self.destroy()
            StartingScreen(self.master).open_file()
        def save(self):
            save_as = open(filedialog.askopenfilename(), "r+")
            with save_as as file_data:
                file_data.write(self.text.get(1.0, END))
```

Similarly, "Editor" inherits from the "Frame" widget and calls the parent constructor from its constructor like done before. A menu is then created that is the top bar shown here with the word "File", once the object is created:

When "File," is clicked on that frame, it presents these options:

This menu is given the "master" parameter so it can be linked to it, and later in the code, the "master" is configured, so that will be the menu. Between the configuration and the declaration of the menu, one menu item or cascade is created called "file." The "file" variable will have some options (commands), which are "New," "Save," and "Exit." These each have their respective label and function. Then finally, it is added to the main menu. Then a new scrollable text widget is created from the Tkinter module. The "content" variable is inserted inline 1—the number the float is indicating—and the widget gets packed into the frame. The frame is then packed into the window.

However, there is still the task of calling of the methods from the commands: "back_to_start" and "save." The "back_to_start" method changes the menu to an empty menu, destroys itself, creates a "StartingScreen" object, and calls the open file method. The "save" method asks the user to open a file accessible in reading and writing mode using the variable "save_as." Then this resource file is opened and replaced with the text from the text widget from line 1 to the "END," a constant Tkinter variable to get the end.

All the classes are now created, leaving only the step of creating the window and object of the "start":

```python
if __name__ == '__main__':
    root = Tk()
    root.title("Notes App")
    start = StartingScreen(root).pack()
    root.mainloop()
```

The final "if" statement checks whether it is directly running because this file can be imported to other projects for its classes and variables. When it is, it must not run this code.

CHAPTER 15:
Future Roadmap

With the knowledge of Python this book offers, it is possible to take your skills further in a specific genre within the wide world of programming and accelerate your journey to become a developer. Learning Python opens many career paths and choices. Numerous open-source libraries are speeding up the process. The below subchapters give a general overview of how to get into a specific genre of programming.

Web Development

The *frontend*, or the user interface and interactions, are powered by HyperText Markup Language (HTML), Cascading Style Sheets (CSS), and—optionally—JavaScript (JS). These skills are required for those who want to pursue web development. *HTML* builds the website's structure, *CSS* styles the website, and *JS* makes the website interactive.

Python comes to play on the server-side, where it updates and deletes data in the database. Typical tasks that Python does on the server-side include authenticating a login, saving data and input from the user, and rendering a page based on the URL to the user. Python frameworks for web development include Django and Flask. A *framework* defines the structure of an application. *Django* is a full-featured but complex web framework, while *Flask* is light and simple. Django provides all the tools for a web application. In Flask, you import only what is needed rather than everything coming with it.

Flask is an ideal learning framework for those getting started with web development. On the other hand, Django is a great framework for those already familiar with Flask. Both frameworks share much in common and require at least some basic HTML and CSS knowledge along with some optional JS.

Data Science

Data science uses data and algorithms to gain useful insights and analytics from data. Python libraries can serve as a tool for data scientists.

Numerical Python (NumPy) is a library that provides powerful tools to work with numeric data. It can also perform complex mathematical operations on a *multidimensional array*. A grid of values is like a multidimensional array; if the grid is on a square, it will have two dimensions, but if it is on a cube, it will have three—and the number of dimensions can keep going. *Arrays* are almost like lists in Python.

Pandas is a tool for data processing, data analysis, and data manipulation using data structures. This library is a powerful tool for working with data.

Matplotlib is a plotting library that creates visualizations of data in the form of graphs and charts.

Machine Learning

Python is one of the most popular programming languages for artificial intelligence. Therefore, it has plenty of opportunities for learning this topic.

Tensorflow is a library built and maintained by Google LLC. This library makes it easy to implement machine-learning algorithms. As the name implies, Tensorflow is full of *tensors* (multidimensional arrays), which makes it easy to create *neural networks* (computer systems that are capable of making decisions).

PyTorch is another machine-learning library aimed at speeding up the development process.

Scikit-learn is another library with a rich feature set for modeling and many other machine-learning algorithms.

Cheat Sheet

Name	Description	In Practice
Print function	Displays string to console	print("Hello World")
Comments	Notes in code that don't execute	#This isn't executed
Variables and Data		
Assigning variables	Allocates a memory location for a name with a value	my_variable = 0 my_variable += 1
Integers	Whole numbers	1, -30, 503
Floating Points (Floats)	Numbers with decimals	3.14, 5.0, 9.3493
Complex Numbers	Numbers expressed as a+bj	10+5j, 1j
Arithmetic Operators	Symbols that denote a function	addition(+) subtraction(-) division(/) floor division(//) multiplication(*) exponentiation(**) modulus(%)
Strings	A series of characters surrounded by either double or single quotation marks	"Hello", 'World'

Name	Description	In Practice
Concatenation	String values joining together	"Hello" + "World", "High Score: " + str(500)
Escape Characters	Escape the default behavior of a character and insert it in the string	double quote(\") single quote(\') backslash(\\) new line(\n) tab(\t)
String Indexing	Characters accessible via their index, starting from 0.	str[0], str[8:15]
Format Strings(F-Strings)	A way to insert data to strings	f"Variable: {variable}"
Booleans	True/false values	True, False
Comparison Operators	Compare values returning a Boolean	==, !=, >, <, >=, <=
Identity Operators	Compare memory locations	is, is not
Membership Operators	Check whether an item is another	in, not in
Logical Operators	Combine two conditionals	and, or

Name	Description	In Practice
Truthy/Falsy Values	Values that have a truthy or falsy value when converted to a Boolean	Falsy Values: Empty strings and collections Values that are 0 False None Truthy Values: Everything else
Lists	A mutable, indexed collection of items	[1,2,3]
Tuples	An immutable collection	(1,), (1,2)
Sets	An immutable, unordered, and unchangeable collection containing no duplicates	{1,2,3}, set([1,2,3])
Dictionaries	A mutable, unordered but indexed collection via keys	{"One":1, "Two":2},
User input	Asks user input after the message is printed.	user_input = input("Enter something:")
Casting/ Constructors	Converts one data type to the other using the special constructor functions	int() float() complex() str() bool() list() tuple() set() dict()

Control Flow		
Name	**Description**	**In Practice**

"If" Statements	Executes its code block if conditional is true
	
	"if" conditional:
	
	    Code
		if True:
		    pass

"While" Loops	Keeps running its code until the conditional is proven false
	
	"while" conditional:
	
	    Code
		i=0
		while i >5:
		    print(i)

"For" Loops	Loops through an iterable	for item in list:
		    print(item)
		
		for i in range(0, len(list), 1):
		    print(list[i])

Raising Exceptions	Outputs an exception or error	raise Exception

Exception Handling	Instead of outputting in except, it will try to do something, but it will run the except block if it fails	try:
		    print(5/0)
		except ZeroDivisionError:
		    print("Infinity")

Functions		
Name	**Description**	**In Practice**

Creating Functions	A block of code that can be called later	def my_function(e):
		    print(e)
		
		def my_function(e):
		    return e
		
		five = my_function(5)

Calling Functions	Executes a functions block of code	my_function(e="Sai") my_function("Sai")
"*args"	Get all the unnamed parameters in the form of a list	def print_all(*args): print(args)
"**kwargs"	Get all the named arguments and puts it in the form of a dictionary, key value.	def print_all(**kwargs): print(kwargs)
Lambda	A single-line function that returns at least one value	ten = lambda: 5+5

Modules and Packages		
Name	**Description**	**In Practice**
Packages	The commands to install packages and libraries can be found in PyPi (https://pypi.org/)	PyPi (https://pypi.org/)
Installing/ Uninstalling Packages	This code goes in the terminal	pip install package pip uninstall package
List of Packages Installed	Views all the packages installed using this command in the terminal	pip list

Importing Packages	Get the methods and variables from another file	from b import b_file_fn
		  b_file_fn()
		
		from b import *
		  b_file_fn()
		
		from b import b_file_fn as b
		  b()
		
		import b
		  b.b_file_fn()

Turtle		
Name	**Description**	**In Practice**
Empty Turtle Screen	The "mainloop" function keeps rendering the window and the code after it will only execute when the window gets destroyed	import turtle turtle.mainloop()
Changing Window Title	Changes the window title	turtle. title("Window")
Changing Background Color	The "bgcolor" method accepts either a color name or a hex code.	turtle.bgcolor("light blue")
Pen Customization	The shapes can include a turtle, arrow circle, and triangle	turtle.shape("turtle") turtle. fillcolor("blue") turtle. pencolor("white")
Going to a Coordinate	Goes to an x and y coordinate	turtle.goto(100, 100)
Going Forward	Goes forward by a certain length	turtle.forward(100)
Turning the Direction	This turns the turtle by a number of degrees	turtle.backward(90) turtle.right(90) turtle.left(90)
Creating a Circle	The parameter of this is the radius of the circle	turtle.circle(50)

Working with Text Files		
Name	**Description**	**In Practice**
Opening Text Files Using Context Managers	This opens the resource, and its code block uses the resource and then it closes it	with open("file.txt", "r+") as file_data: print(file_data.read())
List of Lines	Returns the list of all the lines in "r" (reading)and "r+" (reading and writing) modes.	print(file_data.readlines())
Replacing a File's Content	This replaces all the content in writing mode("w")	file_data.write("Hello World")
Appending to a File	This appends to the file in appending mode("a")	file_data.write("New Content \n")

PYTHON FOR BEGINNERS

Object-Oriented Programming		
Name	**Description**	**In Practice**

Creating Classes	A blueprint of methods and variables	class MyClass:
		  def __init__(self, v):
		    self.variable = v

Private Variables/ Methods	Private variables and methods are hidden from the object by putting two underscores in front of the name	Private Variable: self.__password Private Method: def __fn(self): pass
Inheriting	Borrows parent's methods and variables if not overridden	class Child(Parent): pass
Calling Parent's Methods	The parent is referred to as super and can be used to call the methods	super().__init__(v=1)

123

More Python

Name	Description	In Practice
Iterators	Functions that take an iterable or a class that has an "__iter__" and a "__next__" method and iterate over it	iterator = iter(list) iterator .__next__()

Iterable Classes	When the iterator is created and an object of it is created, it will run its "__iter__" method; every time it is iterated, it will run the "__next__" method.	Methods:
		def __iter__(self):
		    return self.v
		def __next__(self):
		    prev_v = self.v
		self.v += 1
		return prev_v

Decorators	Alter the functionality of a function by adding more computation and finally returning the function's value or executing it	def check_dn(fn):
		    def inner(a, b):
		      if b == 0:
		    return None
		      else:
		    return fn(a,b)
		    return inner
		
		def divide(a, b):
		    return a / b

CPSIA information can be obtained
at www.ICGtesting.com
Printed in the USA
BVHW010734060223
657820BV00047B/955

9 780578 771809